EXPLORING THEATER

Stage Management in Theater

Jeri Freedman

Cavendish
Square

New York

Published in 2018 by Cavendish Square Publishing, LLC
243 5th Avenue, Suite 136, New York, NY 10016
Copyright © 2018 by Cavendish Square Publishing, LLC

First Edition

Website: cavendishsq.com

This publication represents the opinions and views of the author based on his or her personal experience, knowledge, and research. The information in this book serves as a general guide only. The author and publisher have used their best efforts in preparing this book and disclaim liability rising directly or indirectly from the use and application of this book.

All websites were available and accurate when this book was sent to press.

Library of Congress Cataloging-in-Publication Data

Names: Freedman, Jeri.

Title: Stage management in theater / Jeri Freedman.

Description: New York : Cavendish Square, 2018. | Series: Exploring theater | Includes index. | Audience: Grades 7-12.

Identifiers: ISBN 9781502630094 (library bound) | ISBN 9781502634627 (pbk.) | ISBN 9781502630100 (ebook)

Subjects: LCSH: Stage management. | Musicals--Production and direction.

Classification: LCC MT955.F75 2018 | DDC 792.602'3--dc23

Editorial Director: David McNamara

Editor: Fletcher Doyle

Copy Editor: Nathan Heidelberger

Associate Art Director: Amy Greenan

Designer: Jessica Nevins

Production Coordinator: Karol Szymczuk

Photo Research: J8 Media

The photographs in this book are used by permission and through the courtesy of: Cover Photofusion/Universal Images Group/Getty Images; p. 4 Phovoir/Alamy Stock Photo; p. 7 Betsie Van der Meer/Stone/Getty Images; p. 8 Wilf Doyle/Alamy Stock Photo; p. 14 Dean Berry/Photolibrary/Getty Images; p. 16 John Ewing/Portland Press Herald/Getty Images; p. 18-19 Jorge Royan/http://www.royan.com.ar/Wikimedia Commons/File:Dresden – Scenography, set construction and theatrical scenery – 2567.jpg/CC SA-BY 3.0; p. 22, 37 Jim West/Alamy Stock Photo; p. 26 aywan88/Shutterstock.com; p. 28 John Burke/Stockbyte/Getty Images; p. 32 Wavebreak Media/Alamy Stock Photo; p. 39 Al Seib/Lost Angeles Times/Getty Images; p. 42 Gary Gershoff/Getty Images; p. 45 Marc Romanelli/Blend Images/Alamy Stock Photo; p. 47 Cate Gillon/Getty Images; p. 49 Miles Willis/Getty Images; p. 51 Michael Dwyer/Alamy Stock Photo; p. 56 Keith Morris/Alamy Stock Photo; p. 58 Hill Street Studios/Blend Images/Getty Images; p. 60 Jewel Samad/AFP/Getty Images; p. 64 nik wheeler/Corbis Documentary/Getty Images; p. 66 Peter Righteous/Alamy Stock Photo; p. 68 Jonathan Knowles/Stone/Getty Images; p. 72 marvent/Shutterstock.com; p. 75 KeepOnTruckin/Wikimedia Commons/File:Stage managers panel.jpg/CC BY-SA 3.0; p. 77 Rawpixel/iStockphoto; p. 82 Monkey Business Images/Shutterstock.com; p. 84 George Rose/Getty Images.

Printed in the United States of America

CONTENTS

A stage manager reviews the progress of a member of the technical crew.

CHAPTER ONE

The Stage Manager's Skills

The stage manager is, in many ways, the jack-of-all-trades in the theater. During casting and rehearsals, the stage manager assists the director as needed, runs rehearsals, and keeps track of virtually everything. During the staging and performance, the stage manager is responsible for maintaining and **calling** a list of **cues** for the technical aspects of the performance and ensuring that these are executed properly during the show. Stage managers work closely with the director, actors, designers, and technical crew during the entire production process. It is their job to ensure that the show runs without hitches.

High School and Community Theater

In a high school setting, a play is often directed by a teacher or a volunteer. A student is frequently chosen to be the stage manager. As stage manager, he or she assists the director during preproduction activities, helps with rehearsals, keeps track of technical requirements, and conveys the director's instructions to the stage crew. During performances, the stage manager makes sure that the backstage elements are in place and oversees the crew. Stage managing provides an excellent opportunity to learn about all the aspects of a theatrical production. It gives a student the chance to learn what the stage manager does and also to become familiar with a wide range of technical skills, from set design to lighting and sound.

Many cities and towns have community theaters. In some cases, a local group of amateur actors puts on performances in rented or donated venues such as school auditoriums, or town or local organization halls. This type of community theater is often organized by an individual who directs the plays. The group might put on plays on a regular basis all year round or seasonally, such as in the summer or during major holidays like Christmas or Halloween. The group might consist of a permanent group of people who perform or work as stage crew in different productions. In other cases, the director might hold auditions for each play the group performs. The participants in this type of community theater usually work at regular jobs or are retired, and they put on plays in their spare time.

There are also professional community theaters, such as summer theaters, that have a permanent facility and a paid full-time staff. This type of group is headed by a professional director, **producer**, or administrator who hires the actors and crew for the plays that are performed. These organizations might use all amateur actors and crew or a combination of professionals and amateurs. Most are nonprofit organizations, and they often offer classes and internships in addition to performing plays. When a professional community theater hires a professional stage manager, it often has a role for an intern as an assistant stage manager.

Required Skills

The stage manager fills many different roles and works with people in many different specialties. The stage manager is the director's key assistant. He or she works with the actors, scheduling and running rehearsals, cuing actors, acting as **prompter** during early rehearsals, and ensuring that the actors

A stage manager assists the director by running rehearsals with some of the actors.

The stage manager supervises the construction of a set for a play, as well as the teardown.

are in the right place for their entrances during the performance. He or she also works closely with the stage crew. The stage manager acts as a **conduit** between the director and crew, letting the craftspeople—such as set designers, lighting and sound technicians, and wardrobe staff—know what the director wants them to do and coordinating their work. As part of this coordination, the stage manager works with the crew to plan the handling of wardrobe changes, scene changes, sound and lighting, and props. The stage manager makes notes in a copy of the script about key elements of each scene, such as where actors should be located and lighting, sound, prop, and wardrobe requirements. This copy of the script is called the "prompt copy." During the show, the stage manager will cue the technical crew's activities. As with the actors, he or she must ensure that everyone in the crew is in the right place and prepared for each performance. The stage manager is also responsible for supervising the setup and **teardown** of equipment and sets used in the play.

Given the variety of tasks stage managers must perform and the different types of people they must interact with, they need a wide range of skills to succeed. Stage managers require technical skills, organizational skills, and interpersonal skills.

Technical Skills

The stage manager needs to understand a variety of technical aspects that go into producing a play. Although stage managers do not need to be experts in every technical aspect of theater, such as lighting and sound, they need to have a basic understanding of those activities in order to work with the technicians who perform them. There are many books available that provide information on the technical aspects of theater, including amateur productions. In a high school production directed by a teacher, the director will explain what is required. The stage manager will need to learn how to write up a cue sheet and must understand basic rehearsal techniques.

Often the director will run rehearsals with some actors, while asking the stage manager to rehearse other performers. The director of the play will make decisions as to the actors' **blocking** (placement and movement), **stage business**, and the desired emotions, gestures, and vocal expressions. The stage manager must note how each scene is to be performed so he or she can run rehearsals with the actors. One way to learn the technical aspects involved in putting on a theatrical performance is to become a student intern at a professional community theater.

Organizational Skills

Few positions are busier or require engaging in a broader number of activities than being a stage manager. Furthermore, performance dates are set, so everything must be completed by opening night. Getting everything done on time requires excellent planning and organizational skills. Stage managers must keep accurate lists of all technical, backstage, and onstage requirements. They must be able to break the requirements down into specific tasks, communicate the requirements to the crew, and keep track of their progress, ensuring everything is ready when needed. Stage managers must be able to multitask.

In the theater, the unexpected is the rule. Stage managers must be able to think on their feet and deal with problems that arise unexpectedly. They must not become stressed out by the frantic pace of activity. Organizational skills allow the stage manager to manage his or her time and schedule. This means being able to keep track of the technical elements—costumes, lighting, props, scenery, and the like—that need to be completed, and then checking on the activity of the crew regularly to ensure that everything is ready when it needs to be. Stage managers must also have excellent time management skills, which means being able to prioritize everything that needs to be done, then dealing with the most important things first. It may require the stage manager to delegate some of these activities to the appropriate technical staff. Time management skills allow a stage manager to do what needs to be done for the play and still have time for other aspects of his or her life.

Stage managers must pay attention to detail. They are responsible for making sure that props, crew, and cast are where they are supposed to be. A missing prop, a misplaced piece of furniture or **set dressing**, or a missed cue can cause a problem during a performance.

Interpersonal Skills

Much of a stage manager's time is spent working with other people. He or she must tell people what needs to be done and when to do it, and must do so without antagonizing them. Stage managers work with people in a wide range of positions and with different personalities and **temperaments**. Stage managers must be tactful—that is, sensitive to others' feelings. They must be able to correct people without sounding arrogant or disrespectful, and get people to do things without ordering them around. When dealing with the crew, they must explain the director's instructions in a way that encourages cooperation. When rehearsing actors, stage managers must be able to give criticism and suggest improvements without offending or insulting people. Their job is to present criticism with an attitude of trying to help the actor give the best performance possible. Stage managers must have patience with actors and crew who are, after all, volunteers. They must be able to handle frustration and address problems without acting angry or upset. The stage manager sets the tone for the entire crew. If he or she remains calm in the face of a problem, this will encourage others to do so as well.

Stage managers must be reliable and able to work unsupervised. The director relies on the stage manager to assist him or her by seeing that instructions are conveyed accurately. Stage managers may have to work long hours and apply themselves to a task even when they'd rather be doing something else. Various problems are likely to arise when preparing a play. Some difficulties will be technical, and others may be issues involving cast or crew. In the case of serious interpersonal problems, the stage manager will want to inform the director so he or she can deal with the issue, but many problems can be solved by the stage manager alone. Stage managers need to persevere, even when faced with a variety of problems, and overcome obstacles without becoming overwhelmed. Problem-solving skills allow a stage manager to analyze a situation and define possible solutions or alternatives. Even if the director will be the person to make the final decision, presenting the director with viable solutions can save time and make the director's job easier. However, the stage manager must know when a problem or person is getting out of hand and get the director involved.

Developing Stage Management Skills

In high school, you can start developing the experience and background that will allow you to be successful as a stage manager. There are two types of background you will need. The first is general knowledge. When you are working on theatrical productions, you will be involved in plays from different periods of history and different cultures. Even within a single country, people and attitudes can differ greatly. High school English courses can help you learn about literature and the use of language. Learning the rules of grammar and syntax helps you understand how language works. In addition, learning to write and speak clearly and accurately will help you communicate successfully with the cast and crew. Studying history helps you to understand the context in which a play takes place. This knowledge will help you understand what the director is trying to achieve in his or her approach to the play and will clarify the requirements for the sets, costumes, and props.

The second type of knowledge you will need is directly related to the performing arts. If your school has a drama club or a course in drama, you may want to participate as a stage manager or assistant to the person directing the play. If a teacher is directing a school play, see if there is a need for a stage manager to assist with the production. If not, volunteer for other behind-the-scenes work. Doing so gives you hands-on experience, a chance to perform the tasks required to produce a play, and knowledge of

A knowledge of history helps the stage manager understand technical requirements for a historical play.

the terminology of the theater. Many community theaters need help with the production aspects of the plays they perform. Volunteer for behind-the-scenes work or see if the director can use you as an assistant. Community and summer theaters often have positions for interns. Contact the local theaters

in your area and ask if they have student intern positions. These are unpaid positions in which students perform a variety of behind-the-scenes tasks. Larger community and summer theaters often employ professional actors and staff, who can provide invaluable information. Above all, to be a good stage manager, one must be ready to accept a great deal of responsibility. This is something that you can practice while in school by accomplishing the tasks you are given by teachers on time and to the best of your ability, and by correcting any mistakes without making excuses.

The stage manager oversees the setting up of the stage lights.

CHAPTER TWO

Working with a Team

The stage manager works with virtually everyone involved in putting on the play. The stage manager does not have authoritative power as the director does. He or she does not decide who gets which role or who works on what job. In certain cases, such as when conveying direct requests from the director, stage managers have the authority of the director behind them. In most cases, however, the stage manager must get people to do what is required by using his or her leadership skills to motivate them.

The stage manager must keep volunteer crew members working constructively, even when problems arise. Eventually, all stage managers find themselves in a situation where they have to deal with conflict between crew members, or between crew and cast members. The stage manager's skills in handling people will be critical at this point.

The Cast and the Crew

The stage manager works with the cast, the crew, and the director. The director is in charge of managing

The set crew builds, paints, and installs the sets and backdrops for the play.

the cast and crew. He or she chooses the cast and crew members and makes the decisions as to the design elements to be incorporated into the play—including the set, lights, sound, costumes, and so on. The cast consists of the actors performing the play. The crew includes the backstage and technical personnel. The crew might have some or all of the following positions, depending on the size and nature of the play. A high school or community theater may not use

these formal names for its crew members, but it will still need people to perform these roles:

Lighting technician: The person who arranges the lights for the performance and controls lighting changes during the play.

Sound technician: The person who creates and records sound effects and runs them during the play.

Costumer(s): The person or persons who assemble or make the costumes the actors wear. If there are costume changes during the play, a wardrobe person might help the actors make those changes.

Set designer/crew: The set designer creates the plan for the set according to the director's instructions. He or she might also gather furniture used in the play. There will usually be a crew of people who build and paint the set according to the plan.

Prop master: The person who assembles or obtains the required props and sets them in proper locations for use during the performance.

Makeup artist: In many high school and community theaters, actors handle their own makeup. However, for historical or holiday plays, or those requiring special effects makeup, a makeup artist might be employed.

Stagehands: The people who change the sets and furniture, if necessary, for different scenes during the performance.

Building a Team

The stage manager is the person the director relies on to manage the crew as well as to assist in rehearsing actors. The director is extremely busy running rehearsals, working on the design of various aspects of the play, and often handling issues such as advertising and other **front-of-house** matters. He or she counts on the stage manager to be able to work effectively without constantly coming to the director to resolve problems. The stage manager must make sure that the members of the crew are getting their work done properly and on schedule and that they treat each other with respect and work together well.

Getting People to Work Together

Community and high school theater productions employ mostly amateur actors and volunteer crew. Most of these people also have a day job or school responsibilities and/or family commitments to deal with. Since, in most cases, no one is being paid, the stage manager must be able to persuade the crew to show up when needed and do the work that needs to be done.

Members of the crew may come from a variety of ethnic and cultural backgrounds. It is the stage manager's job to ensure that all the people who make up the crew are working together, despite having different levels of experience, different types of personalities, and different backgrounds.

One way to motivate people is to create a sense of **camaraderie**—making people feel that they are all important parts of a team. The stage manager needs to treat crew members as people who can be relied on to help make the play a success, not as **subordinates** who can be ordered around. By emphasizing how

A stage manager often works with crew members from diverse backgrounds.

important each person is to the play, the stage manager encourages each one to feel a responsibility for its success and to make it a priority.

People like to do things that make them feel appreciated and important. The stage manager should give crew members recognition and praise when they contribute useful ideas and do good work. Making people feel valuable encourages them to want to participate and do their best. The stage manager may have to convey changes the director wants, correct mistakes, or ask people to do a better job. Rather than blaming the crew member, a successful stage manager will focus on the problem and emphasize that the stage manager and the crew member are working together to address the issue. This helps to create an atmosphere in which people help each other rather than try to fix blame on each other when something goes wrong.

Likewise, if the stage manager is running rehearsals, he or she should praise the cast when they do a good job or make a positive contribution. This is especially important because the director is likely to ask the stage manager to rehearse the actors with smaller roles while the director works with the main actors. Because these actors are not the stars, they need reinforcement as to the fact that they and their roles are important to the production. This approach encourages actors to support each other rather than compete for attention.

Adding a social element to group work also puts people in a positive mood and makes them feel more like a team. For example, one might order pizza when the crew is working all day on the weekend. Even if everyone has to pitch in to pay for the food, it creates a sense of fun that makes the work less **onerous**.

Handling Conflict

Whenever one is working with a group of people, sooner or later conflict will arise. The stage manager must be able to deal with conflict. The stage manager must be able to discuss problems calmly and constructively, without blaming the person or people involved. People are more likely to cooperate in fixing problems if they are not blamed. If the stage manager sets a positive example by approaching problems and mistakes as something that can be fixed by working together, others in the cast and crew will be more willing to step up and help others in the same fashion. It also makes people more likely to bring problems to the stage manager's attention promptly.

The stage manager does not choose the cast or crew, and even the director may have a limited pool of people to call upon. Therefore, the stage manager must be able to handle people who are temperamental. It's important to give everyone a chance to say what is on his or her mind. Sometimes just listening to a person helps defuse a difficult situation. When dealing with someone with a negative attitude, the stage manager can ask that person to help with a particular problem, giving him or her the opportunity to demonstrate technical expertise. The stage manager should recognize people who come up with solutions to problems and assist others. This can encourage those who want attention to behave in a more positive way to get it.

Occasionally, a confrontation between two people might occur. This might be the result of a disagreement about how something should be done, or the people involved might have personal issues. This type of argument can easily spiral out of control among young people, who haven't learned to control their emotions or to resolve disputes without **acrimony**.

The best time to stop a confrontation is before it gets out of control. As soon as two people start arguing or making nasty comments, the stage manager can interrupt them, asking what the problem is or redirecting their attention back to the project. If the people are willing to discuss the issue with the stage manager, he or she can take them aside to deal with the issue. If it is a disagreement about a technical point, the stage manager can explore the pros and cons of both their views and make a decision on how to proceed. If it is a personal matter unconnected with the play, the stage manager can try to get them to agree to leave the problem outside when they are working, for the good of the production. Alternately, the stage manager can see if one of them can work on some other aspect of the production. If the participants cannot be calmed down or refuse to cooperate, the stage manager will need to have the director intervene. The stage manager should never get between two people who are having a physical confrontation. Instead, he or she should make sure no other people are in the vicinity, where they might get hurt, and then seek out the director or another person of authority to deal with the confrontation.

Balance and Stress Management

Stage managers must record all the technical cues and prompt actors during rehearsal, work with all the crew in preproduction, and make sure everything runs smoothly during performances. All of these activities keep the stage manager very busy. Rehearsals and crew work often take place on several evenings per week and on weekends. While not all cast and crew members need to be present for all work sessions, the stage manager will probably have to be there for most of them. Going to school and being a stage manager requires managing one's time carefully.

Delegation and prioritizing tasks ensure a student stage manager has enough time to study.

The stage manager needs to work out how long the required activities are going to take and how they can be fit into a schedule, allowing extra time for unexpected problems, which always occur. Student stage managers should make a weekly schedule so they know in advance when both school and theater projects need to be done. However, for a student, the educational aspects of school must come first. If time is needed to study for an exam, for example, tell the director. He or she can get another member of the cast or crew to fill in when necessary.

It is important to remember that the stage manager is not the person responsible for the actual implementation of every technical aspect of the play.

There should be a designated person in charge of each technical area, such as lighting, set construction, and costuming. The stage manager should check with those people to make sure everything is on schedule and there are no problems, but trying to manage every detail will mean giving insufficient attention to any one area and will only lead to burnout.

A stage manager cannot afford to get completely overwhelmed and stressed out. No one can do the impossible. The director, especially if inexperienced, may keep asking the stage manager to handle more and more activities. The director might not even be aware of how much work he or she has loaded onto the stage manager's shoulders. It's up to the stage manager to go to the director and explain that it is not possible to do everything the director wants. The stage manager can ask the director to prioritize which activities are most important or to recruit another person to assist the stage manager with some of his or her responsibilities.

To perform well, stage managers must take care of themselves. This means eating a healthy diet, getting enough sleep, and exercising. Working as a stage manager may be demanding, but participating in a theatrical production should also be fun and fulfilling.

A stage manager sits at her station backstage with a headset to talk to the crew and a prompt book.

CHAPTER THREE

Stage Managing the Play

In the production phase, the stage manager is responsible for maintaining the prompt book. The prompt book is a loose-leaf binder that contains the script of the play, including any changes. On the script, the stage manager notes the blocking and stage business performed by the actors in each scene. The prompt book also includes all other documentation and records required for the performance, such as rehearsal schedule sheets and the cue sheet for the technical aspects of the play. The stage manager works closely with the director at every phase of the production process. He or she must be present at the early rehearsals to record the blocking and stage business and to gain an understanding of the director's concept for the performance of the play. The stage manager is responsible not only for letting the actors know when they are needed for rehearsals, but for ensuring they are present when needed as well. These are only the specific duties of the stage manager, however. In fact, the stage manager acts as a general assistant to the director during the preproduction and production phases, and his or her duties will vary from play to play. Stage managers can be responsible for anything and everything. There are three phases to the play production process: preproduction, rehearsal, and show time. The stage manager has different tasks during each of these phases.

Preproduction

There are two major aspects to the preproduction phase: research and planning. Through research, the stage manager gains an understanding of the requirements for the play. The first thing the stage manager should do is read through the script several times to become very familiar with it. The script provides the stage manager with the knowledge of what the production's technical requirements are likely to be. The stage manager thinks about what issues the script might raise. For example, are there key props, scene or costume changes, sound and light effects? Even if the stage manager has worked on a production of the play previously, it's necessary to start from scratch. Every director and theater group has their own interpretation of every play they produce.

The stage manager works with members of the crew. The crew might consist of people who responded to flyers soliciting helpers to work on the play, or they might be contacts of the director, community members, or students who auditioned but weren't selected to act in the play. The stage manager does not design the play. The director does that. However, the stage manager is responsible for keeping track of the technical requirements for the play. Even before the director makes specific design decisions, the stage manager reads through the script and makes lists of the requirements for the sets, lighting, sound, costumes, and props. The lists should include the act, scene, and page number in the script for each required element. As the director works out the exact design of the play, the stage manager updates these lists, which can then be given to the technical crew. The requirements lists will be updated as needed. Examples of items to be included on a list for sets are: "a fireplace with electric fire" if the script calls for a character to burn a note, or "a working window" if the script calls for a character to open one. The lighting list includes light changes, such as those that occur when a character turns a light on or off. The sound sheet includes elements such as the sound of a burglar alarm, a news report being heard from a radio, or the ringing of a telephone.

One of the stage manager's duties is to have everything necessary for each rehearsal ready to go. This means that if a specific costume element, such as a hat or trench coat, or specific props are needed to rehearse a scene, they are available. Sheets listing costume and prop requirements for each scene serve this purpose. Finally, the stage manager should research and note in advance information that actors or crew are likely to need during the production phase, such as a list of foreign words used in the play and their proper pronunciation. The stage manager should become familiar with the customs and manners of the period in which the play takes place, the historical events of the time in which the play is set, and biographical information on any historical characters referred to in the play.

Actors waiting to audition look over material provided by the stage manager.

As the director makes decisions regarding the staging of the play, the stage manager adds additional requirements to the sheets and gives them to the head of each technical area. For instance, the director might make an artistic decision to have the sound of a storm be heard when the window is opened.

Casting

One of the first tasks the director of the play will undertake is casting. Actors are solicited by flyers, notices in local papers and online, email, and similar methods. The stage manager might assist the director in the preparation and distribution of notices that auditions are being held by making flyers and listing the audition information in online and social media sites. If the school or theater has a Facebook page, an audition notice can be listed there as well. The audition notices and flyers will give the name of the play, the location and times of auditions, a phone number to call for more information, and some information about the characters required. If there are specific gender or age requirements, then these are noted. Most plays have characters who can be played by a person of any race or ethnicity, but sometimes a play requires actors with specific characteristics. For instance, a play about black people facing prejudice would require a certain number of black actors. The requirement for actors of a particular background should be specified on audition notices. A notice might say, "Required: one African American male, aged twenty to thirty-five; one African American female, aged twenty to thirty-five; three women, any racial or ethnic background; two young men, any racial or ethnic background." It is a good idea to include on the notice that crew members for lighting, sound, makeup, costuming, or other tasks are also required.

The stage manager might also be charged with setting up the audition space. This includes providing chairs for actors waiting to audition and setting up a table and chair for the director, and for the music director and choreographer if the play is a musical and these professionals are part of the staff. Auditions for school productions are usually held after school. Community theater auditions usually take place in the evening, so people can come after work, or on the weekend.

When actors arrive for the audition, the stage manager presents them with an audition form to fill out with their contact information; physical characteristics such as age, height, and hair and eye color; experience and special skills; and times they are available. The form should also ask if they would be willing to help with the production as a crew member if they are not chosen to act in the play, and if so, what area(s) they would be interested in working in. Some actors auditioning for community theater roles will bring a résumé and/or photograph. The stage manager should have a stapler handy to staple these to the audition form. Actors should also be provided with a schedule of the dates of the play and the general schedule for rehearsals (e.g., Monday, Wednesday, Thursday, 6–9 p.m., and Saturday, noon–4 p.m.). The stage manager should have a smartphone or digital camera to take a picture of each actor (if the applicant does not supply a photo). This helps the director remember who is who when casting. The photos can be printed out and attached to the audition forms.

During an audition, those auditioning for a role are given the script and asked to read the part of the character(s) for which they are being considered. In the case of school and community theater, the director generally just asks the actors to read the dialogue of one or sometimes a couple of characters. After all the auditions are completed, the director will decide which actors are serious contenders for each role. If more than one actor is being considered for a role, the director will hold callbacks. In this case, the director will contact the actors he or she is considering and ask them to return at a specific date and time for a final tryout. The stage manager will prepare copies of the scenes the director plans to use for the callbacks and again organize the space and bring in the actors needed. Sometimes the stage manager will be asked by the director to read lines with the actor being auditioned. After the callbacks, the director will make his or her final cast suggestions. After the director makes the decision as to which actors will be cast, he or she will work out a rehearsal schedule. The stage manager will then draw up a list of all the cast members and the characters they are playing and provide it, usually via email, to the actors chosen, along with a schedule for rehearsals. The people who have applied to be on the crew or who indicated on their audition forms that they would be willing to do so must be contacted. The director may have the stage manager call these people and arrange a meeting to discuss the technical requirements with them and draw up a work schedule.

The stage manager will keep track of the schedule and which actors are needed at a particular date and time. A play with few actors is easier to schedule than one with a large cast. In community theater, where plays might be performed by a small permanent company, it may be difficult to recruit enough people from the community to perform a large-cast play, and the plays chosen often have a small number of actors. For school plays, when there are many students who want to participate, or when the play is chosen for its educational value (for example, one by Shakespeare to expose students to his work), the play chosen might have a large cast.

Preparing for Rehearsals

Before rehearsals get under way, the stage manager needs to become familiar with the facility where the play will be rehearsed and performed, whether this is a school auditorium, a permanent theater space, or a town hall. The stage manager should know where all the light switches are and which lights they control, where the controls for speakers are if they are used, where the thermostat is and how to operate it, where the power outlets are, and where the restrooms are. He or she should locate the fire extinguishers and other safety equipment in case of emergency.

The stage manager is responsible for "calling" the show, or giving cues during the performance. For this purpose, he or she will have a desk or podium placed backstage in a position from which the entire stage is visible. It must be placed where it doesn't interfere with the entrances and exits of the actors. Finally, it will save a lot of trouble if the stage manager maintains a list of key information, such as emergency numbers; a list of restaurants that deliver, with their menus; the numbers of taxi companies; the location of public transportation; and the nearest drugstore.

Production

The key activity during the production phase is rehearsals. A number of furnishings may be required backstage, depending on the play. For example, a prop table is virtually always required so that actors can pick up the objects they carry in each scene. A quick-

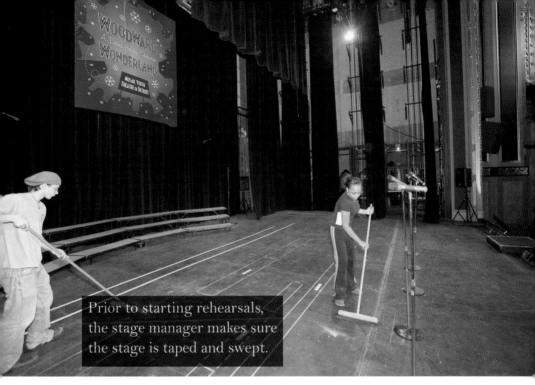

Prior to starting rehearsals, the stage manager makes sure the stage is taped and swept.

change booth or screen may be needed if actors have to change costume and reappear in the same or the next scene. Setups for special sound or light effects, and flats or furniture for scene changes must also be available backstage. The stage manager must arrange a location for all of these objects so that they do not interfere with the movements of actors entering or leaving the stage. Further, these items must not block the stage manager's line of sight because he or she must be able to see what is happening onstage during the performance.

In addition to preparing the backstage area, the stage manager tapes the stage. When rehearsals start, the sets have not yet been constructed, and the furniture will probably not be available. In order for the actors to know where doors, windows, stairs, and furniture will be located, the stage manager measures out spaces in the correct size and shape and creates an outline of these elements with spike tape. This allows the director and actors to work out appropriate movement as if the actual objects were present.

The stage manager needs to draw up a production schedule. This is a chart that lists all deadlines for all the work of the technical departments from initial design through completion. It is given to the crew in each technical area so they have an overview of the technical requirements. The production schedule also includes the dates that **technical rehearsals** and **dress rehearsals** will take place.

Rehearsals

Typically, rehearsals will take place on several evenings or weekends each week for four to six weeks, but the exact number of rehearsals will vary with the size of the theater group, the number of actors in the cast, and the complexity of the play. In high school theater, all of the actors are inexperienced. In community theater, the actors might all be inexperienced actors, all experienced amateur or retired professional actors, or a mix of experienced and inexperienced actors. The latter is the most common situation. The rehearsal phase also requires the stage manager to keep track of all the activities necessary to put on the show. The production period is often chaotic. As rehearsals take place and the play takes shape, technical requirements and choices often change, and the stage manager must constantly update the prompt book and the crew.

Rehearsals typically begin with a read-through of the play by the complete cast. The stage manager

During rehearsals the stage manager makes notes on cues and changes ordered by the director in a prompt book.

usually reads aloud the stage directions during the read-through. At this time, the cast is provided with information about what is expected of them. This is a good time for the stage manager to pass out the rehearsal schedule—if it hasn't already been emailed—and any other information sheets that are necessary, including a list of rules that the actors are expected to follow.

A major part of the stage manager's job during the early rehearsals is recording the blocking— the placement and movement of the actors—as it is established by the director. Accurate blocking information is important for light and sound cues. It is also required for **presets**—the placement of props and furniture when a scene is set up. Blocking often changes during the course of rehearsals, but the stage manager needs to start recording it when rehearsals begin. He or she then alters the notes about blocking as changes occur. For this reason, blocking notes should be recorded in pencil. The stage manager should also make sure that the actors are noting their blocking in their scripts. Otherwise, he or she will have to constantly remind them where they should be. Because the technical aspects of the play—such as light, sound, and props—as well as the actions of other actors may depend on the actors being in the right places, blocking is very important.

There are a number of ways to record blocking. One simple way is to divide the stage into a number of areas and record the movements of the actors from one area to another. For example, a stage manager might divide the stage into six regions: upstage right (UR), upstage center (UC), upstage left (UL), downstage left (DL), downstage center (DC), and downstage right (DR). Left and right refer to the perspective of an actor onstage facing the audience. Downstage is toward the audience, and upstage is away from the audience. When an actor moves from one part of the stage to another, this is called **crossing**. The stage manager makes a note of such a move by writing, for example, XDR, which means "crosses downstage right." In some cases, especially in community theater or outdoor productions, plays are staged on round or roundish stages. In this case, the stage manager will treat the stage either as a compass or a clock, dividing it into compass directions such as N, NE, E, SE, S, and so on, or into clock points such as 12, 1, 2, 3, and so on. Thus, an actor might

XDL3 (cross downstage left to the three o'clock point). The stage manager marks on the dialogue in the script when the actor begins to move in the indicated direction and at what point in the dialogue the actor stops.

During rehearsals, actual sound and light changes do not take place. Instead, the stage manager calls the cues for these events—for example, "The phone rings," or "The lights go out." In the case of sound effects, the stage manager may make an actual approximation of the sound. The advantage of making an actual sound, even if it's not realistic— for example, saying "bang!" for a gunshot—is that it gives the actors a sense of the actual time the sound will take, which makes it easier for them to get their response time correct. It also helps the stage manager get a feel for exactly when to call the technical cues. The stage manager doesn't need to call light cues for subtle changes in lighting that don't affect the behavior of the actors. However, in some cases, the light does affect the action. For example, if a character is breaking into a safe and someone flips on the lights, or if a sudden loss of electricity causes the lights in a room to go off, then the stage manager would call those cues.

Prompting

Prompting means giving a hint to an actor who has forgotten what he or she is meant to say next. Prompting is one of the stage manager's activities during rehearsal, especially at the point when the actors first go **off book** (the script is referred to as

PETER LAWRENCE

Peter Lawrence is a professional stage manager of Broadway shows. His career spans more than forty years, mostly on Broadway, and he has worked at a variety of production-related jobs, including associate director, production stage manager, production

Peter Lawrence holds his Tony Honor for Excellence in Theater.

supervisor, associate producer, production manager, stage manager, and director of national tours. Among the shows he's worked on are *Miss Saigon*; revivals of *Annie Get Your Gun* and *Gypsy*; Neil Simon's *Broadway Bound, Rumors, Lost in Yonkers*, and *Jake's Women*; and *Spamalot*. Lawrence comes from a family of actors and has loved the theater since he was a child. He enrolled in the College of Wooster to study law, but he soon realized that the legal profession didn't interest him and transferred to Ohio State University to major in theater. He had planned to teach stagecraft, but one summer he worked in professional summer theater and decided that was the life for him. He got a master's degree in theater at the University of Hawaii, and then moved to New York.

As a production stage manager or an associate director, Lawrence is responsible for the technical side of the production during the preproduction phase. After the show opens, Lawrence's job changes, and he has to keep the show fresh and alive while maintaining the vision of the director. In 2013, he became the first stage manager ever to receive a Tony Honor for Excellence in Theater. "For a stage manager this is an impossibility—we don't get Tony anything," he says in an article on the Tony Awards website. In an article in *Playbill*, Lawrence states, "The theatre lets you know you're welcome. And once you're welcome in the theatre, it's the best life you can have. I'm the luckiest guy in the world to have been tapped by the theatre."

"the book"). In early rehearsals, the director primarily works with the actors on blocking and the nature of the characters they are portraying. At that point, the actors haven't yet memorized all their lines and read them from the script. In later rehearsals, the director expects the actors to have completed memorizing their lines and starts rehearsing them without their scripts in front of them. Directors like to achieve this point as soon as possible because it allows the actors to interact with each other instead of looking at the script, but it's common for actors to forget a line at this phase.

The stage manager prompts them by giving them a few words of the line. He or she must be careful, however, not to prompt an actor who has merely paused for dramatic effect. To avoid doing this, the stage manager must become familiar with the actors' style of delivery and the **pacing** of the exchanges in the play. Prior to rehearsals, the stage manager discusses with the director the procedure to be followed when prompting actors. For example, the stage manager might prompt an actor only if he or she says "line," which means the actor needs the line. The stage manager needs to follow the text in the script as the actors speak their lines so that the correct line can be supplied immediately, without breaking the mood of the play. The stage manager also takes notes regarding mistakes the actors make with the lines or blocking, but these issues are usually pointed out after the scene has finished, unless they cause a major problem. For example, if an actor changes the phrasing of a line slightly or moves too

A stage manager prompts actors if they forget a line during rehearsal.

soon, the stage manager would make a note of this for discussion after the scene has concluded. If the actor makes a major mistake, such as jumping ahead to lines that occur later in the scene, the stage manager will interrupt and draw attention to this fact. Often, the stage manager will give his or her notes to the director, who will discuss them with the actors at the end of the rehearsal, as the director may already have noted the problems.

If an actor is having difficulty remembering his or her lines, the director may ask the stage manager to spend some time with that actor rehearsing the lines. This process is called **running lines**. When running lines with an actor, the stage manager reads the other characters' lines and corrects any mistakes the actor makes in his or her lines. This process is repeated until the actor has learned his or her lines. The stage manager may also be asked to rehearse other aspects of an actor's performance that require extra effort. For example, when I was interning as an assistant stage manager in a community theater, the director asked me to rehearse an actress who had to sing a song during one scene until she had the delivery down the way he wanted it.

Another responsibility of the stage manager is timing the show. It's important to know how long scenes, and the play, will run. The director will have an ideal time in mind for the length of the performance and the pacing of the scenes. He or she will need the timing information to determine whether the pacing of the scenes is correct. If a scene is taking longer than expected, the actors may not be picking up their cues well or may be performing too much business, stretching out the scene. If the scene is running faster than usual, the actors may be rushing their lines. It's also important that the scenes take about the same amount of time each time they are performed so that sound and light cues occur at the same time consistently. For example, if a **blackout** occurs at the end of a scene, the time it takes an actor to complete his or her final line and actions should be consistent, so the lighting technician can shut the lights down at the correct point. The front-of-house staff will need timing information as well, in order to set intermissions and provide that information to audience members who ask.

Organizing the Crew

The stage manager needs to keep in touch with the heads of all the technical teams working on the crew to make sure that everything stays on schedule. He or she also needs to provide the technical heads with an updated list of requirements on a regular basis. For example, the stage manager needs to keep track of which props are needed in each scene and where they should be placed. Often the director will add or change props during rehearsals. The stage manager records these additions or changes on the prop list and gives it to the person in charge of props. It is useful to take a digital photo of the set with the props in place for each scene. The stage manager also

A dresser waits beside costumes to assist actors with their quick changes.

makes a list of all set change requirements and any set pieces, such as furniture, that need to be moved during scene changes. He or she then assigns crew members to set and move these during scene changes. The stage manager provides the crew members with floor plans showing the location of the set pieces in each scene. He or she may also mark the stage with small pieces of tape to help the stagehands place furniture in the correct location during set changes. This is called spiking the stage; each mark on the stage is called a spike. Different colors may be used to distinguish between scenes.

The costumer will need the actors at various times for fittings. The stage manager must find out when actors will be needed and then schedule them for fittings with the costumer. If the play requires clothes the actors are not used to wearing (as is common in historical plays), or if an actor needs to practice with a piece of clothing such as a hat or cape, the stage manager needs to arrange substitutes that actors can work with while their costumes are being made. For instance, a piece of remnant fabric can be used as a cape during rehearsal. The stage manager gets a list of costume changes from the costumer. Sometimes actors need to make a quick change, meaning there isn't enough time for them to go to their dressing rooms to change. In this case, the stage manager may arrange for a changing booth to be set up offstage and, if necessary, for a crew person to assist the actor. The actor can duck into it, change, and reappear onstage in a few minutes.

As the rehearsal period approaches its end, the stage manager and director will run technical

A cue light allows an actor waiting backstage to see to make his entrance.

rehearsals, in which the lighting, sound, and other technical aspects of the play are practiced. The stage manager might run **dry tech rehearsals**, in which the crew practices the sound and light cues without the actors present. The stage manager might also run **stop-and-go rehearsals**, in which the crew runs a scene or portion of a scene with actors, to practice the cues. In these rehearsals, if a problem occurs, the action is stopped and the scene is rerun. The stage manager makes clean copies of the script with all the technical cues for use in these rehearsals. Sometimes an actor has to make an entrance from backstage into an unlit area. For instance, an actor might be standing backstage behind a door through which she has to enter. In order for her to see her way onstage, **cue lights** might be provided. Cue lights are low-wattage lights that provide enough of a glow for the actor to see where he or she is going. These lights are usually controlled by a **toggle switch** on the stage manager's desk or podium and are flicked on right before the actor's entrance, then off again.

Full Rehearsals

The final week before the show is devoted to full rehearsals. First, there is a full technical rehearsal. At this time, all the technical elements—sets, lights, props, sound, music—are carried out as they will be in the regular performance. The tech rehearsal takes place first, at the beginning of the final week, to allow any problems to be fixed in time for the performance. Prior to the technical rehearsal, the stage manager draws up a comprehensive running list, which includes all the technical elements that will occur during the play, such as the light, sound, costume, and set changes. The stage manager gives the list to all crew members, who can mark the items they are responsible for on their copy. Before the tech rehearsal, the stage manager sets up a table where he or she, the director, and the sound and light designers can view the stage and make notes. The stage manager and sound and light technicians will wear headsets that allow the stage manager to call cues if necessary. The stage manager will have a **god mike**. This is a microphone that can be heard backstage, in actors' dressing rooms, and in other work areas, so that the stage manager can control what happens

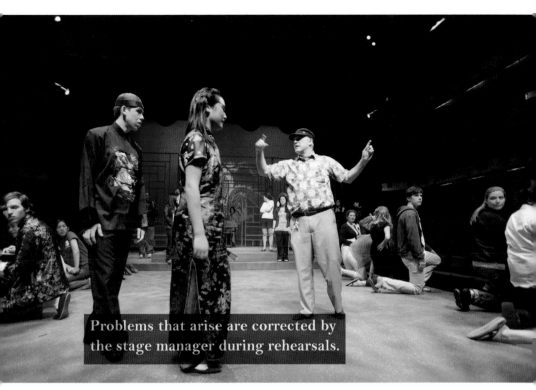

Problems that arise are corrected by the stage manager during rehearsals.

during rehearsals and the performances. The stage manager will see to it that the stage and backstage areas are clean and free from obstacles. He or she will use glow tape to mark any objects the actors might bump into or trip over, and will turn on **work lights**, called **backstage blues**, whose blue glow allows the backstage crew to see during the performances. Throughout the rehearsal period, the stage manager keeps track of the technical cues, marking them in his or her script, using a notation such as S1 for sound cue 1, L1 for light cue 1, and so on. Also included is a page of cues for before the play starts, indicating, for example, the cues for the **house lights** dimming, music starting, the actors taking their **places**, and the like.

During the full technical rehearsal, the actors perform the play as if it were an actual performance. However, the director and stage manager focus on the crew, not the actors. The stage manager makes sure the crew has all the cues down and that the changes work properly. Actors wear (and change) their costumes during the tech rehearsal, providing an opportunity to note if there are any timing problems with costume changes. Typically, many problems occur during the technical rehearsal. When the rehearsal is over, fixes are performed to eliminate the problems. During the full technical rehearsal, the stage manager calls cues over the headset for all the technical aspects of the play as they will occur in the actual performance. Cues are called in three phases: standby, response, and go. The stage manager will say, for example, "Standby lights 1," and the light board operator will respond "Lights standing by." The stage manager will then say "Lights 1 go," and the light board operator will perform the appropriate action.

The next few rehearsals are full rehearsals with tech and actors, culminating in full dress rehearsals. Most directors call for two or three dress rehearsals on the days directly before the first performance. In the dress rehearsal, the complete play is performed exactly as it will be in front of a paying audience. Often the cast and crew are allowed to invite family or friends to the dress rehearsal. Doing so gives the actors the chance to perform in front of a live audience, and the director has the chance to see if the play is having the desired effect. During the dress rehearsals, the stage manager calls cues from the actual podium or booth that he or she will use during the performance. In this way, he or she can see the play from the vantage point used for the actual performance and make any adjustments necessary.

A lot of work is required of the crew during the rehearsal process. The people on the crew in school and community theaters are usually volunteers. Therefore, the stage manager must do what he or she can to make the effort pleasant by giving them the chance to be creative and engage in the process as a social activity as well as work.

Performance

When the play is performed, the stage manager arrives about an hour and a half before the performance is due to start. He or she posts the sign-in sheet, which all cast and crew members sign as they arrive to indicate they are present. He or she makes sure that the crew members, who arrive at this time, are ready and that any tasks they need to do are done. The stage manager has preshow and postshow checklists. Before the show, the stage manager runs through the items on the preshow checklist, including tests of the technical systems. The preshow checklist might be something like:

- Check that the stage has been swept and mopped.

- Check that the backstage areas are properly set up.

- Make sure the cast and crew members have all signed the sign-in sheet, and call any who have not.

PERFORMANCE SIGN-IN SHEET

Stage Manager: _____

Date: _____

Production: _____

Director: _____

NAME	TIME

Actors and crew members sign in to let the stage manager know they are present.

- Check that the placement of furniture and props on the set is correct.

- Check that all props are on the prop table (the table backstage where actors pick up their props before going onstage).

- Run a sound check (test that all sound-making devices are working).

- Run a light check (make sure all the lights are working by having the light board operator turn each on and off).

- Make sure everyone's cell phone is turned off.

- Make sure the backstage lights are off except for work lights.

Thirty minutes prior to **curtain** (start time for the show), the stage manager lets the **house manager** know that he or she can open the house (let the audience in). The stage manager also alerts the cast and crew as to the time to curtain at thirty minutes, fifteen minutes, and five minutes before the show starts. At five minutes before curtain, the stage manager calls the crew to their places. At three minutes before curtain, he or she calls "Places," and the actors take their positions for the start of the play. The stage manager checks that the cast is in place, then checks that all crew members are in place and on headset. Once everyone is in place, the stage manager checks with the house manager to make sure there aren't any delays in seating the audience. If there are, then the stage manager will hold the curtain, or wait,

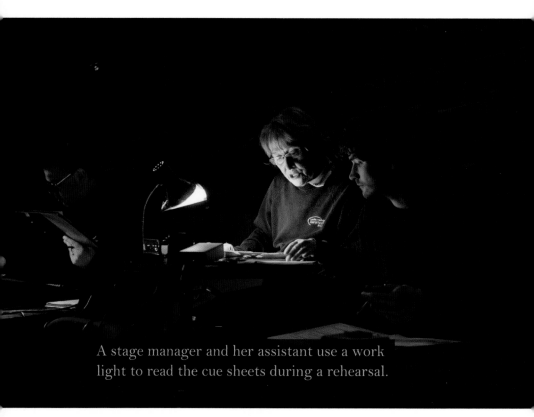

A stage manager and her assistant use a work
light to read the cue sheets during a rehearsal.

a few minutes. In a school play or a small company,
the director may make the decision when to open
the house. The stage manager is still responsible for
seeing that everything and everyone are ready.

During the show, while calling cues, the stage
manager watches the play. He or she makes notes
of anything the actors do or say that varies from
what is set out in the script. In a school play or small
company, the director will watch the performance
from the rear of the theater and take notes. If
there are things the director wants to bring to the
attention of the actors, he or she will tell them
after the performance or before the next evening's
performance. In a larger community theater, the

director will probably be present only for the first performance. After that, it is the stage manager's responsibility to make sure the actors stick to the director's staging and the script. It will sometimes be necessary for the stage manager to correct actors' performances. Before the cast and crew leave, the stage manager makes any announcements that are necessary. These may include, for example, notes about the performance or a reminder that the show the next evening will start an hour earlier.

The stage manager maintains a postshow checklist that covers everything that must be done after the performance. This list generally includes such tasks as having the prop crew or assistant stage manager sweep and mop the stage, making sure all the props are accounted for, checking that no costumes need to be fixed, and returning any valuables that have been locked up for the actors during their performance. The checklist even includes notes to turn off the lights in the restrooms and lock all the doors.

The stage manager discusses with the actors issues that arose during the previous performance.

CHAPTER FOUR

Pitfalls and Problems

All types of problems can arise during the preparation and performance of a play. Some types of problems can be anticipated. Other problems are unpredictable. As you might imagine from the breadth of the stage manager's responsibilities, he or she is likely to be the person faced with dealing with a large number of these problems. Each play will have its own unique issues. However, there are some typical challenges that arise in the course of producing a play.

Canceling and Rescheduling

One general problem that can happen is the need to cancel a rehearsal or performance of a play. Rehearsals might need to be canceled because of the illness or injury of a director or actor, or because of external issues such as weather conditions. Rehearsals might also need to be changed if, for example, an actor scheduled to rehearse has an emergency. In this case the director might choose to rehearse a different scene in which that actor is not needed. Another situation that can arise, especially when rehearsing a

Extremely bad weather, such as a blizzard, may require the cancellation of a play.

school play, is that the location where the rehearsal is scheduled to take place is needed for another activity. Performances of plays are rarely canceled, but this can occur if there is a major catastrophe such as a blizzard or a hurricane, or a power blackout.

If a rehearsal is canceled or changed, the stage manager will need to contact all cast and crew members and inform them of the change. If a performance is canceled, in addition to contacting the cast and crew, it will be necessary to inform ticket holders. This can be done with a combination of approaches, such as a recorded phone message that people get when they call the theater, a post on the theater's Facebook and Twitter accounts, a notice given to the local TV station that is listing cancellations, and a physical notice posted at the venue where the play was to be performed. If a recorded message is used, it should include instructions on what to do to get a replacement ticket or refund.

Problems with the Cast and Crew

Sometimes the stage manager will have to address problems with cast or crew members. The best approach is to take the person aside. Embarrassing a person by calling him or her out in front of other people will only make the problem worse. Problems with cast and crew should be approached in a nonconfrontational way. Tell the person that you understand he or she has other responsibilities, then explain why it's important to show up on time or do whatever else is at issue. Take a collaborative approach, asking the person what is required to help him or her fix the problem. Get the person to agree to what is necessary so that you can later point out that he or she agreed to this. If the problem persists, it may be necessary to discuss the problem with the director, who can take firmer measures.

Another problem is having an actor drop out of the show. If this happens, the director might be able to contact one of the other actors who auditioned and replace the lost actor. If there aren't any suitable replacements, the director may do another round of auditions. In this case, the stage manager will have to perform the same tasks as in the original auditions, in addition to keeping the crew moving forward with the technical requirements for the play. Once a replacement is chosen, the director may ask the stage manager to spend extra rehearsal time with the new actor to bring him or her up to speed. Community and school companies rarely have understudies—the number of performances is small, so the understudy probably wouldn't get a chance to act. However, the director must rehearse two actors for the part if there is an understudy. If a last-minute substitution must be made close to or during the performance period, and the replacement actor does not have time to learn the lines, he or she may need to carry a script onstage. This is preferable to canceling the performance, but the stage manager may be called on to run lines with the replacement to help him or her memorize the lines quickly.

It's common for cast and crew members to come up with questions as they go through the rehearsal process. Often they will have questions for the stage manager when they arrive for rehearsal. If this happens, talk to one person at a time, and give that person your complete attention. If you can answer the question then and there, fine. If you can't, don't guess or give an off-the-cuff reply. If your guess turns out to be incorrect, this can result in a problem, or at least confusion, later. Instead, say you don't know, but you'll find out. Make a written note so that you remember to find out the answer. When you know the answer, inform the person. Always carry a small notebook with you. That way, you can write down any questions or issues that need to be addressed. You can then follow up with the answer as you promised. This approach will not only ensure that issues don't go unaddressed but also make the members of the cast and crew feel that you can be relied on to get them the information they need.

It is possible for an actor or dancer to be injured during a rehearsal or performance. Before beginning rehearsals, the director and stage manager should work out a **protocol**, or series of steps to be taken, in case of emergency. In addition, a list of emergency contact phone numbers, including the local ambulance company, fire department, and police department, should be prominently posted backstage. Once the actors are cast, ask if any have medical problems that might need to be addressed. For example, a person who is asthmatic might have an asthma attack and need to use an inhaler with medication. Make the other members of the cast aware of the problem so they don't panic if a problem occurs, and make sure that you and the director know what medication the actor might need and where it is located. It is useful, in life as well as in the theater, to take a course in cardiopulmonary resuscitation (CPR) and first aid. Such courses are given by organizations such as the Red Cross and the American Heart Association.

One of the stage manager's responsibilities is to see that whatever rules the director or theater has in place are followed. Such rules cover issues such as "no food anywhere but in the break room." In a community theater, this might mean "no smoking inside the theater building." Most theater groups have a rule that visitors are not allowed to attend rehearsals—except the final dress rehearsals in some

A stage manager discusses with visitors the rules for observing a rehearsal.

cases. This is an important rule because it keeps the rehearsal space a place where actors feel comfortable. They can try out bits that might fail or make mistakes with their blocking or lines without fear of embarrassment. All such policies should be included on a sheet distributed and explained at the first read-through. The sheet should also be given to crew members as they come on board.

Despite this, it's not unusual for members of the cast or crew to want to bring friends or family to watch them work. If this occurs, the stage manager may need to intercede and explain that they cannot do so. If the director is in the theater, the stage manager can tell the director of the problem. However, if the director has not yet arrived, the stage manager may have to run interference by reminding the actor of the policy and asking his or her friends to respect the other cast members' privacy and wait somewhere outside the rehearsal space.

If the actor objects, discuss the matter with the director when he or she arrives. Enforcing the rules means that the stage manager might not be popular with everyone. However, that is part of being a manager. Your first duty is to the play, and that means that you have to be the protector of the other actors.

The stage manager doesn't have to be tough all the time, however. He or she can do things that enhance the actors' and crew's experiences in little ways, such as making sure that bottled water and soda are available and giving thank-you notes to cast and crew at the end of the run.

Technical Problems

Running tech means dealing with mechanical equipment and electronic devices. As you probably know from real life, anything that can go wrong with a device will go wrong—sooner or later. For this reason, all members of the technical crew should check and test their equipment—such as lights, sound devices, and props—prior to each performance. This alone will not prevent problems from occurring, however. Light bulbs burn out suddenly, fuses blow, and wires come loose.

One type of problem that occurs is a missed technical cue. The stage manager calls a cue and nothing happens. This might be the result of a crew

A lighting technician uses a light board to control the stage lights.

member not hearing the call or not paying attention, or it might be due to a mechanical failure, such as a loose wire. When this happens, the important thing is not to panic. Find a workaround. If the cue is for a plot-significant event, such as a doorbell ringing, the stage manager might check if the crew member is in place and aware that he or she was cued. If the crew member missed the cue, he or she can do it immediately. If the problem is technical, the stage manager might be able to find a way to create a similar sound, such as by ringing a bell. Sometimes the actors themselves will cover by saying something like, "Wasn't that the doorbell?" If a spotlight that is supposed to follow a singer doesn't work, the lighting board operator can be instructed to turn on some of the regular stage lights at a low level so the singer can be seen. Later, the stage manager will find out why there was a problem and fix whatever is wrong so that it doesn't recur. It's important for the stage manager to remember that the audience doesn't know what was supposed to occur, so as long as the result is acceptable, the audience will remain unaware of the problem.

The stage manager must maintain a good relationship with the cast and crew. Even if someone makes a mistake during a performance, the stage manager should not blame that person for problems when discussing what happened with the director. Instead, stage managers should let the director know they are aware of the problem and either know what caused it or are in the process of finding out and will ensure it is fixed.

Opening night can be a particularly stressful time for the stage manager. Performing before a live audience that reacts to what they see onstage is a different experience for the actors than performing in an empty auditorium. They may change their pace in response to laughter or other reactions from the audience. Also, the crew might have trouble hearing the stage manager call cues if the audience's responses are loud. Therefore, the stage manager might have to adjust the timing of his or her cues.

Keeping Up Morale

The stage manager is an easy target for frustrated crew members and actors. If something goes wrong,

STAGE MANAGING DISASTER

Stage managers have to deal with many types of problems when a play is being performed. Many can be solved with a little resourcefulness. Sometimes, however, the problems are potential disasters. In a 2016 interview in the *San Antonio Express-News*,

Special effects can present special problems.

stage manager Susan Breidenbach talks about the worst problem she ran into while stage managing a show—an experience she had during an Alamo City Theatre production of *Into the Woods*. The show used pyrotechnics in the form of fireworks that were seated in tubes set in holes drilled in the floor of a revolving set. During one performance, an actress kicked one of the tubes, knocking it out of position. Neither she nor anyone else realized this. When the button for the pyrotechnics was pushed, instead of shooting into the air, the firework caused the area beneath the stage to light up. The set was constructed of muslin over a chicken-wire frame and was in danger of catching on fire. Breidenbach picked up a fire extinguisher, walked onstage while the cast froze, pointed it down the pyrotechnics hole and used it, then continued walking off the stage. To be certain that the fire was out, she crawled under the stage unseen, checked, and then crawled back out, while the show went on.

a crew member is likely to be upset and frustrated and snap at anyone around, including you. It's also easy to fall into the trap of feeling you are responsible for everything. In one sense, this is true because the stage manager is the overseer of the production. However, many problems that arise are beyond your control. When fuses blow or lights burn out, or needed materials are not available, these are problems that need to be fixed, but they are not your fault. A stage manager needs to be able to step back and not take things personally.

If someone snaps or shouts at you, don't shout back. If the director, an actor, or a crew member is upset, let the person talk, make sure you understand the problem, and assure the person that you'll address the issue. Then do what you can to fix the problem. Handling problems this way will gain you the respect of the director, the actors, and the crew. No matter how upset the other person is, a stage manager should never say anything nasty to anyone involved in the production. In order for the production to succeed and to keep everyone working as a team, the stage manager must remain calm and keep a positive attitude. The company, especially the crew, is going to follow the lead of the stage manager. If the stage manager is negative, upset, or angry, cast and crew are going to react the same way, so managing attitude is as important as managing the technical aspects of the production.

Keeping a sense of perspective is important. No matter what happens, you are only putting on a play—you are not facing a life or death situation. Dealing with problems is not fun. However, stage managers, especially novice stage managers, need to realize that each challenge they encounter is a learning experience. Not only will you know how to fix the problem the next time it arises, but you will also learn how to handle problems—and problem people—in real-world situations.

Above all, the stage manager needs to keep in mind that one of the most significant tasks he or she performs is to maintain the morale of the company. This means being fair when dealing with problems between actors or between actors and crew. It also means remembering to thank crew members and praise their work to show you appreciate their efforts.

Some stage managers eventually become producers, managing the entire play.

CHAPTER FIVE

Life After Stage Management

Some stage managers remain in that profession until retirement. Others move into other production-related areas, becoming production managers, directors, or producers. Many stage managers work for some years in the field and move on to nontheatrical careers. The skills learned as a stage manager transfer well to a wide range of careers, including business, event planning, travel and hospitality, sales, and other fields in which extensive planning and customer interaction are an integral part of the job.

Stage managers have excellent management skills in general. Therefore, they are equipped to handle pretty much any company management job. One job for which they are well suited is project management. In project management, the manager is responsible for all aspects of a single product or product line. He or she works with personnel in a variety of departments, including development, production, sales and marketing, and finance. Stage managers are organized, have excellent communication skills, and are used to meeting deadlines. Beyond this, they are good motivators and problem solvers.

However, because stage managers don't have corporate business experience, they may find it hard to get a job in general business management. They often find it easier to get hired in an area such as corporate events management. Private event and party planning are also areas in which former stage managers can use their management skills in a creative environment. Sales is another profession that uses the stage manager's skills. Salespeople for companies are on the road a lot of the time, dealing with potential customers in other companies. The ability to read and handle people serves them well, as does being able to present products in the best light. Salespeople have to be well organized and work independently as well as keep track of detailed information about customers and products—skills that stage managers have honed. In addition to practical skills, being a stage manager gives you confidence in yourself and your ability to handle problems and lead people, which is a key factor in being successful in any field.

Pursuing a Theatrical Career

If you decide that you want to undertake a professional stage management career, you will most likely want to pursue a degree in theater arts, stage management, or production management at the college level. If you want to work in Broadway, **off Broadway**, or professional summer or regional theater, you will need to join Actors' Equity, which is the union for actors and stage managers. Membership provides you with information about the field and

Your high school experience could lead you to the work station of a stage manager at a major theater.

contacts with professionals. Interning or obtaining a summer job as an assistant stage manager at a professional theater can provide you with a chance to work with a professional director, stage manager, and cast. Most likely you will begin your professional career as an assistant stage manager. Some stage managers began in specific technical positions, such as working on a light or stage crew. Then they advanced to assistant stage manager, and then stage manager. The knowledge you gained in community or high school theater can be applied directly in your new role, especially your skills in dealing with actors and crew members, and this experience will help you advance in the field.

Real-World Careers

Most people who work in community theater groups do so part-time and work at a regular job in a business or profession. The skills you develop as a stage manager are the same skills needed to succeed in any nontheatrical profession. Therefore, working as a stage manager can help you hone your skills in a way that will benefit your career. The following are some of the ways they can be applied.

Leadership Skills

In any job, you will have to deal with superiors, coworkers, subordinates, and clients or customers. Working with a cast and crew—especially volunteers, who are not being paid to put up with you—teaches you the skills to motivate people. The techniques that make you successful when working with subordinates and coworkers are the same ones that made you successful with cast and crew members. Among these techniques are recognizing and praising people for their contributions, and criticizing them constructively in a way that focuses on fixing the problem, rather than chastising or embarrassing them in public. Work is a collaborative effort outside as well as inside the theater. If the people you work with feel that you respect them and value their contributions, they will be more likely to support you and do their best work for you.

A person in any line of work today must be able to work and communicate with a diverse group of people.

The key to being a successful leader in a business is being able to build a team from a diverse group of individuals. Leadership in business, as in the theater, is about making individuals work together for the good of the project. You will often have to deal with people who have strong personalities and an even stronger desire to gain recognition and advancement. It is your overall vision for a project, and your ability to motivate people to embrace it, that will make a project successful. You must be able to imbue team members with the belief that they must all support and help each other for the project as a whole to succeed. This is exactly what a stage manager must do in a theatrical production.

In business, as in the theater, one has to deal with people in a wide range of jobs and from various educational, ethnic, racial, and socioeconomic backgrounds. A stage manager has to understand, communicate with, and get the best work from people with different skills and backgrounds, while maintaining a sense of **empathy**. In addition, the people skills one gains as a stage manager give one a better understanding of clients or customers. This understanding allows you to identify what they want or need, which in turn can assist you in making sales and establishing long-term relationships with clients. One of the key elements of success in business is the ability to communicate clearly and effectively.

Stage managers have to work with people who are sometimes annoyed, frustrated, angry, or arrogant. In the real world, you sometimes have to cope with difficult people as well, including superiors and customers or clients. As a stage manager, you should have developed the skills to calm a person who is upset about an issue and refocus the conversation on how to solve the problem. Stressful situations arise in businesses when deadlines are tight and problems occur. No one has more experience in dealing with this type of stress than a stage manager.

Budgeting Skills

As a stage manager, one has a certain amount of money available for the technical aspects of the production. The stage manager must keep track of expenditures and find ways of meeting the technical requirements without exceeding the budget. Budgeting is also a key part of business and professional activities. When managing a business, department, or project, you will have to make a budget and ensure that the activities required do not exceed the amount of money available. This will require tracking the expenditures of those who are performing the project tasks and finding a way to deal with needs that cannot be met with the existing allocation.

There are generally ways to deal with a component of the project that are similar to those used in a theatrical production. Therefore, you will be familiar with strategies for addressing financial issues when they arise. For example, you might revise that component of the project so that it is done differently or on a smaller scale, or you might try to obtain more money from senior management (in the theater, the producer). Most school and community plays are produced on a shoestring. The ability to get the desired results with a limited amount of money is a valuable skill that allows a project manager to accomplish a lot with few resources.

Project Management Skills

Whether you are employed in a business or run your own, you will need to manage projects in the real world. Setting up and directing a project for a business or professional undertaking is very much like stage managing a play. You must analyze the requirements for the project and identify what resources and people are needed. Then you must gather those resources. You will need to organize people in various departments to carry out the tasks required for the project, including people who do not report directly to you. You will need to break down the project into discrete tasks, create a schedule showing when each task must be completed, and then schedule people and resources. You will need to provide the people with deadline information and keep track of progress on each task to ensure that everything is ready on time. As in the theater, requirements may change over the course of the project. These changes mean the manager must adjust the schedule, update the personnel involved, and arrange for any additional resources. Stage managers have excellent experience in this type of project management, which is exactly what they do in the theater.

Time Management Skills

Time management skills are critical for getting things done. Stage managers constantly work under time pressure. The show will go live on a set date, and everything must be done by then. The curtain goes up at a set time for the performance, and problems must be resolved by then. Deadlines are inflexible. Stage managers constantly multitask. These factors mean that the stage manager must learn time management techniques. Time management begins with making a to-do list with all required tasks and ranking them in order of priority. One of the major problems with many managers is their refusal to delegate responsibilities and their insistence on controlling how all the tasks involved in a project are done. Stage managers, however, are used to assigning tasks to different experts on the crew and supervising them at a higher level by keeping track of their progress in general. In the business world, where many managers don't give employees this level of freedom, delegation not only allows more tasks to be accomplished simultaneously but also leads to more contentment and loyalty among employees because they feel trusted and empowered. A stage manager knows that unexpected problems always arise, and extra time needs to be allocated to deal with them.

Like a stage manager, a business manager faces a constant barrage of interruptions, questions, distractions, and requests for help from those working on various technical areas. Like stage managers, business managers must address people who are late or who don't show up, who are disorganized or unprepared, or who engage in other actions that disrupt the flow of work. Yet the manager must still pull the entire project together for a successful performance.

Time management also means scheduling time for yourself and your other commitments. In business as in the theater, it is easy to let the job become your whole life. It is necessary to make time to balance the demands of work with those of family, school, or other activities, and to take care of yourself.

Putting on a Show

Sometimes ex–stage managers will find themselves in a situation directly reminiscent of putting on a play. In the business world, you may find yourself putting on presentations to customers, clients, or senior management. You may be asked

FROM STAGE MANAGER TO REAL ESTATE AGENT

SMNetwork.org is a website for stage managers. Among its ideas for possible careers for ex–stage managers is becoming a real estate agent. One respondent who had become a real estate agent indicated that many of the requirements for success in this profession are similar to those possessed by stage managers. Some of the aspects that these two careers have in common are the need for outstanding people skills and time management skills, and the ability to remain calm in difficult situations.

Setting up an open house as a real estate agent requires the same skills a stage manager needs to run a show.

Beyond this, being a successful real estate agent requires the ability to set up the property to be shown, the way one would set a stage, to give the desired impression. Both stage management and being a real estate agent require dealing with irregular work hours and a continuously changing group of people. As in the theater, it's necessary to stay in touch with people—in this case, potential buyers. In many ways, selling real estate and being a stage manager both require one to put on a show, although the former consists of many small shows rather than a single big one, and the amount of money one makes is larger.

to participate in creating events for customers or clients, or representing the company at a booth in a trade show exhibit. The event can be as small as an open house for a property for sale or as large as a corporate conference with hundreds of customers or clients. The process of producing a special event is very similar to the process of producing a play. You will need to establish the requirements for the "performance," acquire the necessary resources, and see that the necessary people, in the form of staff or vendors, are in place. The process involves planning all the aspects of the event, hiring all the vendors and

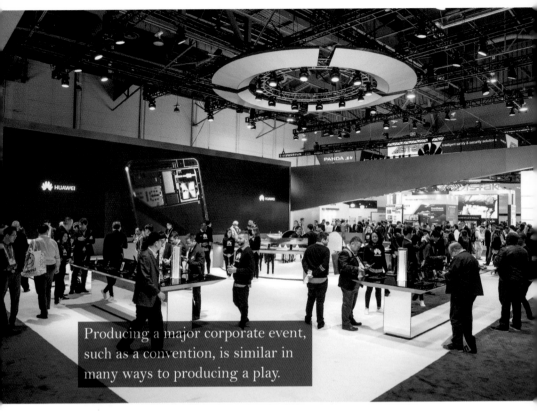

Producing a major corporate event, such as a convention, is similar in many ways to producing a play.

equipment required, and overseeing the production of the event. If the event includes speakers or performers, you will need to make sure that they are accounted for, that they arrive when they are scheduled to, and that they are properly prepared for their performance, just as with actors in the theater.

The Ability to Overcome Obstacles

Stage managing a production means doing whatever needs to be done with whatever resources are available. In a school or community theater, the stage manager must work with the people who are available to act and to do the technical work. He or she must work with the materials that are available to make sets and scenery, costumes, and lighting and sound effects. This approach requires the stage manager to be flexible and adaptable.

The stage manager must be able to evaluate the characteristics and talents of the people who make up the crew. This allows the stage manager to determine who needs what level of guidance and supervision. This ability to use the resources at hand to the best effect possible is invaluable in business. In business, one can't always choose who is working on a project, but one can analyze what team members' strengths are and how to employ them to the best advantage.

Finally, being a stage manager gives one experience in working hard for long hours. The stage manager arrives at the theater first and leaves last. As in the theater, successfully completing projects and meeting goals often means long hours, especially as a deadline approaches. Once the project is completed, like the cast and crew, the team members disperse, and preparations begin for the next effort.

Being a stage manager is a creative and fulfilling job. One has the opportunity to bring all the pieces together to create a successful show. This can create a great deal of satisfaction, despite the hard work required. It is also an excellent way to learn a range of skills that can be used to enhance your performance in a business or profession.

GLOSSARY

acrimony Bitterness or harshness that exists between people or groups.

backstage blues Work lights that allow crew members to see backstage during a performance.

blackout Suddenly turning off all lights to mark the end of a scene or passage of time; this also allows the stage crew to change sets.

blocking The movements and positioning of actors onstage.

call To give a verbal signal or cue.

camaraderie A feeling of good will toward other team members.

conduit A pipeline, or a means of transmitting or distributing.

cross To move from one part of the stage to another.

cue A signal for a cast or crew member to perform an action.

cue lights Low-wattage lights that are turned on backstage to allow actors to safely enter the stage and then turned off.

curtain The time the play starts; it is called this because traditionally theaters have a curtain that opens or rises to indicate the start of the play.

dress rehearsal A type of rehearsal in which the play is performed from beginning to end just as it will be in performance.

dry tech rehearsal A type of rehearsal in which the crew practices without actors.

empathy The ability to understand what other people are feeling.

front-of-house The area where people who handle the administrative and business aspects of the theater, such as box office and publicity staff, work.

god mike A microphone worn by the stage manager that can be heard by the crew backstage and in the actors' dressing rooms.

house lights The ordinary lights in an auditorium or theater.

house manager The manager responsible for overseeing the administrative aspects of a theater and supervising the ushers, ticket takers, and other workers.

off book Reciting memorized lines, not reading from the script.

off Broadway Professional theatrical productions put on in small theaters in New York City.

onerous Something requiring so much effort as to be burdensome.

pacing The tempo, or speed, of a scene or performance.

places Where the actors stand at the start of a scene.

preset The setup of the furniture and props prior to the start of a scene.

producer The individual responsible for the financial and administrative aspects of a play.

prompter Someone who gives a hint to an actor who has forgotten a line.

protocol A series of steps to be followed.

run lines To read lines with an actor so the actor can memorize a part.

set dressing The objects other than furniture that are placed on a stage.

stage business The gestures and activities an actor performs while onstage, such as combing his or her hair.

stop-and-go rehearsal A type of rehearsal in which a scene or portion thereof is rehearsed with actors so that the technical aspects of the show can be perfected.

subordinates Workers who are of lower position than the person managing them.

teardown The process of taking apart and stowing the set and objects used in a play.

technical rehearsal A rehearsal in which the focus is on tasks performed by the crew.

temperament The emotional characteristics of a person.

toggle switch A switch that has two positions: on and off.

work light Blue lights that allow the crew to see backstage during a performance.

FOR MORE INFORMATION

Books

Bailey, Diane. *High School Musicals: Stage Management and Production*. New York: Rosen Publishing, 2009.

Campbell, Drew. *Technical Theater for Nontechnical People*. New York: Allworth Press, 2004.

Kincman, Laurie. *The Stage Manager's Toolkit: Templates and Communication Techniques to Guide Your Theatre Production from First Meeting to Final Performance*. Burlington, MA: Focal Press, 2013.

Roth, Emily, Jonathan Allender-Zivic, and Katy McGlaughlin. *Stage Management Basics*. New York: Routledge, 2017.

Ward, Elizabeth. *Cue Tips: A Stage Management Handbook for High School Theatre*. Rio Rancho, NM: Petals and Pages, 2006.

Organizations

Actors' Equity
http://www.actorsequity.org
The union for actors and stage managers provides news and guidance to its members and those interested in joining.

American Association of Community Theatre
https://www.aact.org
This organization for individuals involved in staging plays at community theaters provides a wealth of information on events such as festivals as well as how to run a show.

Educational Theatre Association
https://www.schooltheatre.org/advocacy/national/organizations
For anyone wanting information on a wide range of organizations, programs, and events that promote theater education in schools, this site is a treasure trove.

Videos

Careers at the National Theatre: Stage Manager
https://www.youtube.com/watch?v=Sj6tvqQR5iw
National Theatre Discover provides a glimpse of all the jobs needed to be done at the National Theatre in London.

Stage Management: How to Call a Show

https://www.youtube.com/watch?v=wRUt269hOq8
This lecture given at a Jacksonville State University Stage Management class takes you through a production and how a stage manager calls the shots.

Stage Manager Calls Cues for Hairspray

https://www.youtube.com/watch?v=5TXBqdDAXgE
Listen to what the crew members hear on their headsets as stage manager Mark Stevens calls the cues for the San Diego REP's production of the musical *Hairspray*.

What's in a Stage Manager's Prompt Book (aka SM's Bible)

https://www.youtube.com/watch?v=TvuQwLv3QUs
Nicholas Acciani takes you on a tour of his prompt book.

Working in Theater: Stage Management

https://www.youtube.com/watch?v=PtLHHAdzAtg
This video, which is part of the Center Theatre Group's Working in Theater web series, allows students to experience the chaos that is the life of a stage manager.

INDEX

Page numbers in **boldface** are illustrations. Entries in **boldface** are glossary terms.

ABOUT THE AUTHOR

Jeri Freedman has a bachelor of arts degree from Harvard University. She is the past director of the Boston Playwrights' Lab, an organization that produced original plays in Boston, Massachusetts. Her play *Uncle Duncan's Delusion* was published by Baker's Plays (now part of Samuel French), and her play *Choices*, cowritten with Samuel Bernstein, was staged at the American Theatre of Actors in New York City. She is also the author of more than fifty young-adult nonfiction books.